*For my sister, Bernie
and her children, Lhara, Michael and William*

ACKNOWLEDGEMENTS

Some of these poems have appeared in *The Salmon*, *Writing in the West* (Connaught Tribune), *Cyphers*, *The Poetry Ireland Review*, *The Honest Ulsterman*, *Gown Literary Supplement*, *The Simon Anthology*, *Bad Seeds*, *The Irish Socialist*, *Oxford Poetry*, *Die Horen*, *In Galway*, *Rhino' Ceros*, *Maryland Poetry Review*, *Visions*, *Ambit*. A selection of these poems have been recorded for 'The Poet's Eye,' RTE television.

The author wishes to thank Mary and Bernard Loughlin of the Tyrone Guthrie Centre, Annaghmakerrig, Newbliss, Co. Monaghan.

And thanks to Lourda D'Arcy of *The Copy Bureau* for the 'o' in Gertrude.

◆ ◆ ◆

DATE DUE	DATE DUE	DATE DUE
20. MAY 94	04 OCT 96	06. DEC
04. JUL 94	02. DEC 96	31. MAY 02
01. OCT 94	12. FEB 98	25 FEB 2017
05. NOV 94	11. NOV 98	22 AUG 2018
28. MAR 95	12. FEB 99	
21. APR 95 28. SEP 95	20/2/99 8/3/99	
15. APR 96	17. JAN 00	
09 07. 96	28. JUN 00	
	17. JAN 05	

First published in 1988 by
Salmon Publishing, Galway

This edition by Salmon Publishing Limited in 1993
A division of Poolbeg Enterprises Ltd,
Knocksedan House,
Swords, Co. Dublin, Ireland.

**Salmon Publishing Ltd receives financial assistance from
the Arts Council/An Chomhairle Ealaíon.**

A catalogue record for this book is available from the British Library.

ISBN 1 897648 08 1

Cover photograph by Gillian Buckley
Cover design by Poolbeg Group Services Ltd
Set by Mac Book Limited
Printed by The Guernsey Press Limited,
Vale, Guernsey, Channel Islands.

Contents

Men with Tired Hair   1

It's All Because We're Working Class   2

Secret Lovers   5

The Ratcatchers   6

She is not afraid of Burglars   8

The K.K.K of Kastle Park   10

It wasn't the Father's Fault   15

The Did-You-Come-Yets of the Western World   16

Be Someone   18

Old Soldier   20

His Mother was the Problem with His Veins   21

I'm Strictly a Chair Person   24

Witch in the Bushes   25

Anything is Better than Emptying Bins   29

Second Thoughts   31

He Fought Pigeons' Arses, Didn't He?   38

I Went to School with You   39

Oracle Readers   41

End of a Free Ride   46

The Tell Tattler   47

No Bliss in Newbliss 49

Woman's Inhumanity to Woman 50

The Blanket Man 52

The Barmen of Sexford 53

Dog is Dog is Dog 56

No Balls at All 57

Sly Autumn 59

Peter Picasso 60

Some People 62

Daughter of the Falls Road 64

Men with Tired Hair

On a bank holiday Monday in Galway,
you can see old men
sitting on window sills in Prospect Hill.

Time is not a factor here,
only images pleasing and displeasing
to the men with tired hair.

Despite this easiness with life,
there is a waiting, a look out
in anticipation of something.

The looking up and down continues;
the awaited stimulus always comes.

Days it's a young woman.
Streets it's a fire.
Years it's news of a tragedy in far off Dublin.

It's All Because We're Working Class

(for Michael A.)

Through them
you could see
no rhyme reason
or gable end;
that coal bag washer
and grass eater
from the Shantalla clinic
prescribed them.

Burn your patch
he said
and be a man;
slip these on
and see into
the souls of men;
and our Ambrose
walked into
the gable end
and his life
was in splinters
thereafter.

All he really needed
was to rest his lazy eye
for a few months
and the wrong eye
would right itself.

It's like having your leg
tied behind your back
for six years
then suddenly have it released
and be told,
go now and breakdance
on a tight rope.

It's all because we're working class;
if we lived up in Taylor's Hill
with the coal bag washers
and grass eaters,
do you think for one minute
they would put
them big thick spy glasses on your child?

Not a tall
not a fuckin' tall;
they'd give ya them film star glasses
with the glitter on them,
just as sure
as all their metallic purple wheelbarrows
have matching cocker spaniels
they would;

fuckin' coal bag washers
and grass eaters
the whole fuckin' lot of them; and
it's all because we're working class.

Secret Lovers

They choke
spare minutes,
burgle glances,
burn each other
with hot
passionate kisses,
miss each other
painfully.

When they meet
in the band room
they fall
to the floor
in a snake-like embrace.

Neither of them
smoke, drink,
or drop acid.

The Ratcatchers

(for Christy)

Their flexible
and benevolent teeth
shine all the way
to Crock-well.

They are related
however distantly,
they will help
they will save him
from the mire,
he may well fall
but it will not be in muck
not while they have
a distant cousin claim on him.

They don't see
that his enemy
has him by the scruff,
for all their books
and their fact full eyebrows
and their jaws full of greasy hope.

When they call
he will tell them
through the slit in their genes
down to their

distant cousined tailshirts,
that he will be
man enough
to get help for himself
when he can no longer
tell his own front door
from the rats
who dance in his pockets
until then,

he will drink on.

She is not afraid of Burglars

(for Leland B.)

It's lunchtime
and he's training the dog again.
He says to the dog in a cross voice,
'Stay there.'
The dog obeys him.

When he goes home
he forgets to leave the cross voice
in the green where he trains his dog
and spits out unwoven troubles
that won't fit in his head.

He says to his wife,
'Stay there.'
His wife obeys him.
She sees how good he is with the dog
and how the dog obeys his cross voice.

She boasts to the locals,
'I would never be afraid of burglars
with my husband in the house.'

The locals, busting for news, ask her,
'Why would you never be afraid of burglars
with your husband in the house?'

She calls a meeting at Eyre Square
for half three that Saturday.
Standing on a chair, wiping her hands
on her apron, she explains.

'One day,' she says, in a cross voice,
'The dog disobeyed my husband
and my husband beat him across the head
with a whip made from horse hair.

That is why I am not afraid of burglars
with my husband in the house.'

The K.K.K. of Kastle Park

At a K.K.K. meeting
in Kastle Park
you could
walk into a dark garden
void of roses
or an after-Easter lily
but reeking with thorns,

briars too
that smoked
and choked
with shouts of
'Get them out,
we don't want them,
they're dirty,
cut off their water.'

These briars
have big brothers
and heavy-bellied husbands
(who are really thistles)

who know only
about foam-backed carpet
and curtains
that go up and down
with a string.

These prickly thistles
have roots
in other parts of town,
where they never saw
foam-backed carpet
or curtains
that went up and down
with a string.

Now these deep roots
spoke often
at peak thistle times
about the lessers
who are dirty
on the outside,

of them they warned,
'My prickly sons,
you are better
than this sort,

so if they cross
your path
step on them
nip them in the bud,
know you are superior.'

And the thorny briars
who smoked and choked
had cacti problems
with their male thistles

and with money
and with awkward-shaped light bills.

Sometimes these thistles
chased other briars;
some played cards
with the briar money
others played the horses
the evil ones drank jungle juice.

All the time
the anger
of the frustrated briars
and thistles
was building up
under the stairs
in the houses
with the foam-backed carpet
and the curtains
that went up and down
with a string.

And the
heavy-bellied husbands
of the thorny briars,

sent out
in the dead of night
their children,
to inform
all the other

briars and thistles
about the Midnight Court at Kastle Park,

where they would
nip in the bud,
the lessers
their fathers spoke about
at peak thistle times.

And all
the under-stair anger
burst forth
and was spread unevenly
over the streets
and over the caravans,

and a chalice full
seeped into
a hive-shaped chapel.

After that
all the thistles and briars
went home
and danced
on their foam-backed carpet,

and pulled the string
and the curtains
came down and down
(but no one took any notice).

And they all
slept soundly
knowing they did a good job,
nipping the lessers
in the bud.

It wasn't the Father's Fault

His father
him hit
with a baseball bat
and he was
never right since.

Some say
he was never right
anyway.

Standing
behind the kitchen table
one Sunday before Mass
his mother said,

If Birdie Geary
hadn't brought
that cursed baseball bat
over from America,

none of this would have happened.'

The Did-You-Come-Yets of the Western World

When he says to you:
You look so beautiful
you smell so nice—
how I've missed you—
and did you come yet?

It means nothing,
and he is smaller
than a mouse's fart.

Don't listen to him ....
Go to Annaghdown Pier
with your father's rod.
Don't necessarily hold out
for the biggest one;
oftentimes the biggest ones
are the smallest in the end.

Bring them all home,
but not together.
One by one is the trick;
avoid red herrings and scandal.

Maybe you could take two
on the shortest day of the year.

Time is the cheater here
not you, so don't worry.

Many will bite the usual bait;
they will talk their slippery way
through fine clothes and expensive
perfume,
fishing up your independence.

These are
the did-you-come-yets of the western
world,
the feather and fin rufflers.
Pity for them they have no wisdom.

Others will bite at any bait.
Maggot, suspender, or dead worm.
Throw them to the sharks.

In time one will crawl
out from under thigh-land.
Although drowning he will say,

'Woman I am terrified, why is this house
shaking?'

And you'll know he's the one.

Be Someone

(for Carmel)

For Christ's sake,
learn to type
and have something
to fall back on.

Be someone,
make something of yourself,
look at Gertrudo Ganley.

Always draw the curtains
when the lights are on.

Have nothing to do
with the Shantalla gang,
get yourself a right man
with a Humber Sceptre.

For Christ's sake
wash your neck
before going into God's house.

Learn to speak properly,
always pronounce your ings.
Never smoke on the street,
don't be caught dead
in them shameful tight slacks,

spare the butter,
economise,

and for Christ's sake
at all times,
watch your language.

Old Soldier

He stood
at the top
of Shop Street
cursing de Valera
and he muttered
something about
the Blueshirts
and when he saw
Mrs Flanagan, he said,
'You could have
got worse than me,
but you wanted
a fisherman didn't ya?
I wasn't always
like this,' he said,
and his veins broke
and he died alone
but not lonely,
for many's the revolution
he fought in his scullery
with his newspaper
and his fine words.

His Mother was the Problem with His Veins

He wasn't old
but he couldn't
walk properly,
he tumbled
and stumbled
into other people's
dessert.
He fell into aftertalk
after dinner;
he talked about
after things
and after hours
and after mammy dies.

He wasn't old
his mother was the problem with his veins,
she tied them in knots
before he left the house;
she knew in her vein tying heart
that he wouldn't get far,
no race was ever won
by the afterman
with his veins in a twist.

Her reasons were simple.
The fruit of my womb

don't leave me Johnny,
you've had fifty-five birthdays
(but only ten birthday cakes).

Don't grow out from me Johnny,
fruit of my womb,
be in at ten o'clock
and we'll have a look
at your veins.

Stop thinking Johnny
I have a bed full
of thoughts in my head
take from me,
I am your mother
your love
the one who ties your veins
for you.

And after that
all Johnny ever had
were more afterthoughts
about afterwords;

until one day
his veins started to bulge
from the side of his neck
the back of his knees
the ankles
around the curve
of his spine.

And he had a forethought
one evening after eight
about after mammy dies
about after mammy dies.

And he killed her
in his heart,
but he still stumbled
he often fell
he was still an afterman
meddling
in other people's afternoons.

And then she really died
dead dead died
into the ground died
late at night died
into the afterworld
she crawled after dark;

leaving the fruit
of her womb
after her,
now sixty-two
still an afterman
looking for birthday cakes
and a woman
to tie up after him.

I'm Strictly a Chair Person

(for Dr. R.D.)

Dear Doctor,
I have been trying
to reach you,
but every time
I try to ring
your door bell
your savage Alsatian
goes for me.

I wonder
if the fact
that I am
carrying an armchair
has anything to do with it.

My problem doctor,
it's nothing really,
I get emotionally involved
with chairs and things.

I'm not ill or anything,
but I know an awful lot
of sick chairs.

P.S. When we meet, is it o.k. if we stand?

Witch in the Bushes

(for Padraic Fiacc)

I know a man
who tried
to eat a rock
a big rock
grey and hard,
unfriendly too.

Days later
he is still grinding,
the rock
is not getting
any smaller.

Because of this
rock in the jaw,
this impediment,
the man has become
even more angry.

No one
could look at him,
but a few
hard cases did.
They were mostly dockers;
they reckoned,

'We have seen
the savage seas
rise over our dreams,
we can look
at a bull-head
eating a rock'.

The years passed
slowly and painfully,
until one day
the rock was no more,
neither was much of the man.

He didn't
grind the rock down,
the rock
hammered a job
on him and his ego.

Then, one day
an old woman
came out of the bushes
wearing a black patch
and a questionnaire,
in her wand hand
she held a posh red pencil,
well pared.

She questioned him
between wheezes
(she had emphysema
from smoking damp tobacco
and inhaling fumes
from her open fire
in the woods)
if all that anger
for all those years
was worth it.

Old Rockie Jaw
couldn't answer
he had forgotten
the reason
and the cause.

He concluded
'Anger is o.k.
if you spill it,
but chewing
is assuredly
murder on the teeth.'

He had learned
his lesson
he would
pull himself together
smarten up like,

turn the other cheek,
he would go easy
on the oils that aged him.

Every now and then
he weakened,
he let the voice
from the rock take over,
an army voice
with a militant tone,

'A man is a man
and a real man
must spit feathers
when the occasion arises.'

Like all good voices
this one
had an uncle,
it was the voice
of the uncle
that bothered him,
it always
had the same warning,

'About
the witch in the bushes,'
it said,
'Watch her,
she never sleeps.'

Anything is Better than Emptying Bins

(for Jessie)

I work at the Post Office.
I hate my job,
but my father said
there was no way
I could empty bins
and stay under his roof.

So naturally,
I took a ten week
extra mural course
on effective stamp licking;
entitled
'More lip and less tongue.'

I was mostly unpleasant,
but always under forty
for young girls
who bought stamps with hearts
for Valentine's Day.

One day a woman asked me
could she borrow a paper clip,

she said something about
sending a few poems away
and how a paper clip
would make everything so much neater.

But I've met the make-my-poems-neater-type before;
give in to her once,
and she'll be back in a week asking,
'Have you got any stamps left over?'

Well I told her where to get off.
'Mrs. Neater-poems,' I said,
'this is a Post Office
not a friggin' card shop,
and if you want paper clips
you'll get a whole box full
across the street for twenty pence.'

Later when I told my father,
he replied,
'Son, it's not how I'd have handled it,
but anything is better than emptying bins.'

Second Thoughts

It is better
not to tell
your best friend
that you have
a lover.

Because
in fourteen days
you might say
to yourself,

I should not
have told her.
Then you will go
to her house

even though
your shoes
are hurting you,
you will say to her,

my best friend,
remember
what I was telling you
fourteen days ago
at half past five,

well it's not true
I made it up
just for fun,
so forget
I ever mentioned it.

But when
you get to her house
you find
she is not in
in fact
you find her out.

So you go
to her place of work
she works
at the sausage factory.

People
in a small group
at the main gate say,

'She is not here
and you
can't find her in
when she is out,
you must
find her out.'

They tell you this
in a sing song way
she has gone
to the doctor's

they say it
four times
for no reason.

You wonder
if she
has told them,
you wonder
if they
are looking at you funny
and when you pass
are they saying
to themselves,
in their
older sisters' dresses,

'There she goes
that slut,
she should be
in the sausage factory,
she should be
a sausage.'

By the time
you reach the doctor's
she has left,
you are sweating
on the road
through your clothes
into your
tight fitting shoes.

You wonder
if keeping your secret
has made her sick
and that is why
she is
at the doctor's.

You take the bus
to her house
you are there
before she opens
the front gate,

you are disappointed
when her mother
tells you
through their squint window
that she has gone back to work

to make up
the time

she lost
whilst going
to the doctor's
for a prescription
for her father's
catarrh.

You decide
there and then
to take out an ad
in the local paper,

telling her
to forget all you said
that Saturday
fourteen days ago
at half past five.

She is
more than pleased;
to your face
she tells you
the next time
you meet,

she adds to this
without blinking
that you won't mind
if she goes out
with the man

you never
had the affair with
as he had been
asking her
for seven months.

And you
look round the town
you have dragged
your dirty linen through

from her house
to the sausage
to the doctor's
to the mother's

And
you
look
up
and
down
the
long
narrow
streets
of
the
town
you

were
born
in
and
you
wonder.

He Fought Pigeons' Arses, Didn't He?

And she pissed
in his toilet
and ate his sausages
and he said
there was nothing
but lust between them.

And on his day off
he got an aerosol
and he wanted to spray
the arses of dead pigeons black.

And he said to her
'If it's war you want
I'll give you war.
We'll have our own war,
spraying the arses of dead pigeons black
and we'll fight seven days out of six.

And the seventh day of the six
we'll discuss the situation,
and I'll bet you
twenty black pigeons' arses
there'll still be nothing
but lust between us.'

I Went to School with You

My children call her
Dolly Partners
and I don't check them.

Sometimes
when I'm well fed
and satisfied in ever other way
and they say it,
we all laugh.

One night when I was coming home
from Mick Taylor's, half pie-eyed,
she called me.

She had no pies in her eyes
and no flies either
she spoke with her finger
her index finger,
but she never danced with the afternoon
the sunny afternoon.

'It's your duty as a mother
to control your children,'
said the finger, the index finger.

'When you are out
(which is often,' she muttered under her manacles)
'I can hear nothing
but Madonna blaring and your youngest swearing.'

'And furthermore,' said another voice,
in an Italian accent (but we couldn't hear it)

'You miserable hag,
you never speak with your finger
your index finger,
and shame on you
you often dance with the afternoon
the sunny afternoon.
How dare you, how absolutely dare you.'

After that the finger came back on duty,
it was the index finger
and it was night duty
and it was her duty.

And the killing part of it all is, it said,

I went to school with you.

Oracle Readers

And we saw
what we saw
and we didn't see
what was hidden,

and we saw
that they were close,
they did everything
and nothing in unison,

they went for walks
they had talks
they went for tea.

Everyone
who sees them says,
'Look at the O'Hallorans
they are so cute,
would that we were them.'

Once when they
were painting
the house
he got red paint
on his face,
he splashed her
so they would
look alike.

Everyone thought
they were cute,
we all said it together
at the crossroads,
'Aren't they cute
oh so cute
would that we were them.'

Then one night
forty-eight of us
crept up
to their bedroom window.

We heard him say
to his wife
his similar wife,

'Can I come inside you
tonight love?'
And she said
in a soft voice
in a similar voice,

'No dear,
not tonight dear,
three weeks
from now dear.'

We were conned
by their cuteness,
they were not
as cute
as we thought.

After that
we wised up,
no longer
did we stand
at the crossroads
and shout,

'Aren't they cute
oh so cute
would that we
were them.'

Our tune changed,
now we said,
'They fooled us
they fooled us,'

we were cocksure
he came inside her
every night
but he didn't,
three weeks
from now dear.

We were fooled
we were conned
learn from us
and read
the signals correctly,

if a man splashes
red paint
on his wife's cheek
it means

he wants to come inside her;
if she leaves
the paint on
and smiles at him
all that same day,
that can mean
everything and nothing.

You think
that means yes,
we have a surprise for you,
oracle reader,

the word
no for nothing
is forming
in her brain
and in her mouth,

while she is looking
at the stars
in his eyes
this no good,
no for nothing
will sneak out
and devour him.

Remember this
and learn
to interpret the paint splash,
and don't
get your signals
mixed up
at the crossroads,
like us
who thought we knew.

End of a Free Ride

For years
my cousin never charged me
on the bus.

One day he said to my sister,
'Your wan would need to watch herself
stickin' up for the knackers.'

After that he went home
and had pigs cheek and cabbage,
lemon swiss roll and tea.

He called out to his wife Annie
(who was in the scullery steeping
the shank for Thursday)

'Annie love get us the milk,
was I tellin' ya,
I'll have to start chargin' my cousin
full fare from here on in.'

'Why's that?' said Annie love
returning with the milk.

'Cos she's an adult now, that's why.'

The Tell Tattler

Have you anything
to tell us today
tell tattler?

Did you help any
old woman across
a crowded street?

Did you spread
your Sunday coat in muck
for any dainty foot?

In a pub
spacious enough
for dreamers with hope,
not near enough
to Annaghmakerrig,
you can meet the tell tattler
with a gold pelican pinned to his lapel.

Without coaxing
or pain he will tell you
about the blood he has given over the years.

He was a school teacher once.
He put streams of children into his wife,
but they fell out again uneducated and sour.

In time they shouted
from sinking Monaghan hills,
'Where is our blood giving father now,
our chest pounder and coat spreader?
We no longer see his polished pelican
shining in the distance.

Your falling out children need to check;
that you have tells to tattle,
that you have an endless supply
of unwilling old women to drag across busy streets,
that you have cloth enough for the dainty foot,
that you have good hearing for when the bell tolls,
that you are not, our father, running out of blood.'

No Bliss in Newbliss

I searched for the heart of Newbliss.

'Would ya?'
said the man with the hat
to me in the pub in Newbliss.

'Would yourself?'
said I to the man with the hat
in the pub in Newbliss.

'I asked you first,'
said the man with the hat
to me in the pub in Newbliss,

'It's my prerogative to be late,'
said I to the man with the hat
in the pub in Newbliss.

'Who said anything about marriage?'
said the man with the hat
in the pub in Newbliss to me.

Woman's Inhumanity to Woman

(Galway Labour Exchange)

And in this cage, ladies and gentlemen,
we have the powers that be.

Powder power,
lipstick power,
pencil power,
paper power,
cigarette in the left hand power,
raised right of centre half plucked eyebrow, Cyclops
power,
big tits power,
piercing eyes power,
filed witches' nails power,
I own this building power,
I own you power,
fear of the priest power,
fear of the Black n'Tans power.

Your father drank too much power,
your sister had a baby when she was fifteen power,
where were you last night power,
upstairs in your house is dirty power,
the state of your hotpress power,
the state of your soul power,
keep door closed power,
keep eyes closed power,

no smoking power,
money for the black babies power,
queue only here power,
sign only there power,
breathe only when I tell you power.

No pissing on the staff power,
jingle of keys power,
your brother signs and works power,
ye have a retarded child power,
you sign and work power,
look over your shoulder power,
look over your brother's shoulder power,
I know your mother's maiden name power,
look at the ground power,
I know your father's maiden name power,
spy in the sky power,
spy in the toilet power,
fart in front of a bishop power.

Apologise for your mother's colour hair power,
apologise for your father's maiden name power,
apologise for being born power.

The Blanket Man

He calls
in his
new Volvo
collecting
the pound a week.

Him and his Volvo.

Sometimes
if she can't pay
he says,
'C'mon, c'mon missus,
if it was my stuff
I'd let you have it
for nothing.'

Leaning against
the door jamb
she doesn't
believe him.

Her and her cigarette.

The Barman of Sexford

In March
Sexford
can be as cold
as any
disappearing relative
with a toothache
you may find yourself
not siding with
in a hurricane.

The barmen
have no problem
with the cold,
they rip off your tights
with their fast
Indian bread breath,
never stopping
for traffic or history.

The people here
are warm
but black tights
mean only one thing
to the men
of Sexford
the barmen of Sexford.

When you
clear your throat
here
the barmen
think
you are addressing them
they say,

'Were you
calling us just then
Black Legs,
can we
do anything for ya,
can we
shine yer knees
please, please?'

The comfort
here
tumbled out
in hot whiskies
and a backbiting fire.

In Sexford
the fire was always there
but the barmen
didn't really exist
only in their mothers' prayers

and in Communion photos
on the dusty mantle
beside the dead president
who was leaning against
the Sacred Bleeding Heart
and of course
in some kind old headmaster's
estimation.

Dog is Dog is Dog

'Xadore, come here,
Xadore, don't urinate there,
not there, not anywhere here.'

If that heap of failure
with the varicose face thinks
that us canines have
the same urinary tract
as those two leggers
she's got another thing coming,

                         on her ankle.

'Xadore, you stupid boy,
come here at once or you will fry.'

Xadore exits to greener lamp-poles.

No Balls at All

The cats in Castle Park
are shameless,
they talk dirty all night long;
but not our Fluffy.

Our cat had been de-railed,
(that's Czechoslovakian for neutered)
but he doesn't know it.

He gets flashbacks
from his desire-filled past;
often along our back wall
he tiptoes tamely chasing pussy;

when he gets to the point of no return
he gets a blackout,
he well knows with his acute cat sense
that the next bit is the best bit,
but he just can't remember
what he is supposed to do.

He was an alley-cat-and-a-half once,
but felines complained,
not softly but oftenly
about his overzealous scratchy nature;

so we took him to the vet
where his desire was taken;
snapped at, whipped off, wiped out
by a man in a white coat.

It was sad really,
de-railed in body but not fully in mind;
would he ever get over it,
our cat with some desire and no equipment?

Days now
he just sits
inside our white lace curtain
envying his promiscuous alley-cat friends.

Other times,
he plays with a ball of blue wool
or a grey rubber mouse
throwing him in the air
letting on to be tough.

Still, he would have his memories,
they would come and visit him
teasing him back
to the tumbling times of testiclehood;

but sadly for the de-railed alley-cat
there is no second coming;
we came to accept it, and so did our Fluffy.

Sly Autumn

Sly Autumn
crept up my skirt
today
in Mainguard Street.

Peter Picasso

Feeding on
potatoes and onions
and heating himself
from stolen coal
and migraine memories
of a day flush with
carrot-weight friends
and apple song,
this Protestant painter lives.

'Take out someone's appendix
make someone's teeth sing
design a hideous church,
but for the love and honour
of all that is holy
stay away from the evil easel,
that's only for the death-coloured
do-fuck-all dandified doters
who'd cut off your ear
as quick as they'd look at you.'

Peter Picasso
who could well hear
but didn't listen
let his brush take him

to this chicken shite wall world
next to Moo-hat post office,
where the crows ate the priest.*
His fall is broken
and so is his heart
when an art student in tight jeans
meanders through his chicken shite world.

He conjures her up
before and after feeds
and provided it's not too wet
and she swears not to step on his wolfhound,
she can glide with him
in and out of the heads of cows
and more things less political.

And on cold winter nights
she can dance
on his stolen coal fire,
while he laughs at the walls
and checks that both ears are still there.

* A Christy Higgins line.

Some People

(for Eoin)

Some people know what it is like,

to be called a cunt in front of their children
to be short for the rent
to be short for the light
to be short for school books
to wait in Community Welfare waiting rooms full of smoke
to wait two years to have a tooth looked at
to wait another two years to have a tooth out (the same
                                                    tooth)
to be half strangled by your varicose veins, but you're
198th on the list
to talk into a banana on a jobsearch scheme
to talk into a banana in a jobsearch dream
to be out of work
to be out of money
to be out of fashion
to be out of friends
to be in for the Vincent de Paul man
to be in space for the milk man
(sorry, mammy isn't in today she's gone to Mars for the
weekend)
to be in Puerto Rico this week for the blanket man
to be in Puerto Rico next week for the blanket man
to be dead for the coal man
(sorry, mammy passed away in her sleep, overdose of coal

in the teapot)
to be in hospital unconscious for the rent man
(St. Judes ward 4th floor)
to be second hand
to be second class
to be no class
to be looked down on
to be walked on
to be pissed on
to be shat on

and other people don't.

Daughter of the Falls Road

In memory of Mairéad Farrell,
murdered in Gibraltar, by SAS
6 March, 1988.

And the world heard
about the awfulness of it
and it got into
the minds of the people.

And it was bigger than them
and they feared it
they feared the bullet
and the bomb,
but mostly their own thoughts.

And in the minds of some people
were thoughts of pity
for the mothers of the three,
thoughts of anger
about the bullets to their heads,
and fear for their own flesh and blood.

And people wondered
why they were there,
and what strength of thought
propelled them, what conviction.

Some said,
tell me now
the politics of the dead,

some mentioned the struggle,
and others said,
the sun shines, we see no war,
but the Irish rarely
feel the sun;
they've heard about the war.

And from the eyes of her brothers
tumbled acid tears,
passing the place of their heart
seeping into closed fists,
and there was an acid tear ocean there
doing nothing. Waiting.

And in the minds of some people
came her mother and father,
they waited ten years,
now ten lifetimes won't bring her back.
Dead daughter of the Falls Road.

And there was talk
she had a boyfriend
who was tall
whose acid tears tumbled
passing the place of his heart,
seeping into closed fists

and there was an acid tear ocean there
doing nothing. Waiting.

And in the minds of a lot of people
was an Irish girl
and her two companions,
brought home in boxes
made from Spanish trees.

And the living don't think
in tall straight lines
and Birch means little
when you're breathing
and in the hearts of some people
came another great wave.

And a lot now hate the Spanish trees
and the great hard Rock
the pitiless Rock
stealer of Irish youth.

By the same author

Goddess on the Mervue Bus
(Salmon Publishing, 1986)

Philomena's Revenge
(Salmon Publishing, 1992)

Goddess & Witch
(Salmon Publishing, 1990)

Face Licker Come Home
(Staged by Punchbag Theatre Co., 1991
& published by Salmon Publishing, 1991)

God-of-the-Hatch Man
(Staged by Punchbag Theatre Co., 1992)